Farrand Press
50 Ferry Street
Isle of Dogs
London E14 9DT, UK

© 1988 Farrand Press

ISBN 1 850830134

British Library Cataloguing in Publication
Data
Sanderson, A.
    Smallpox is dead.
    1. Man. Smallpox. Vaccination 1760–1967
    I. Title
    614. 5'21
    ISBN 1 85083 013 4

Typeset in the UK in Baskerville 16pt by
The Lavenham Press Ltd.
Bound by The Lavenham Press Ltd.
Printed on Fineblade

SMALLPOX
IS
DEAD

by
Arnold Sanderson

illustrated by
Sue Harrison

FARRAND PRESS 1988
LONDON

DOCTOR EDWARD JENNER became one of the greatest doctors in the world because he discovered the first vaccine, how to make it, and how to use it. Vaccines are a way to cure many diseases.

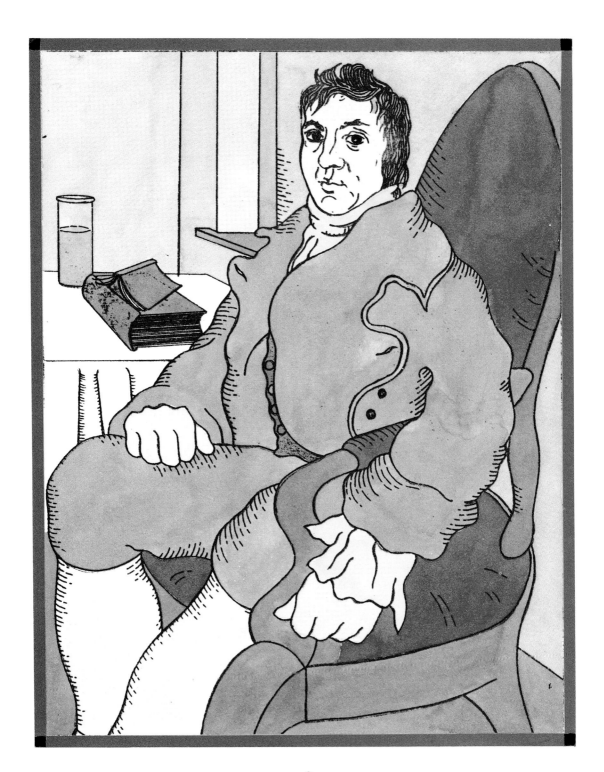

Edward Jenner lived nearly 200 years ago in a small town called Berkeley in England. In those days everyone was afraid of a dreadful disease:

SMALLPOX.

People with smallpox were covered in nasty spots and it made them very sick. Most people caught smallpox at some time in their lives. Many of them died from it. Those who didn't were left with ugly scars from the spots.

When Edward was a young doctor in Berkeley a milkmaid came to see him. She had a spot on her hand. He said it might be smallpox, but the milkmaid surprised him. 'Oh no, doctor,' she said. 'It cannot be smallpox, because I have already had cowpox'. Milkmaids often caught cowpox. Although it gave nasty spots to cows, if a person caught the disease from a cow, it was not very serious. They had only a few spots that did not hurt much and soon went away.

For nearly 20 years Doctor Jenner kept thinking about what the milkmaid had told him. He noticed that other milkmaids seemed never to catch smallpox. They always had clear and smooth skin unmarked by spots or scars. There is even a nursery rhyme about it.

'Where are you going to my pretty maid?',
'I'm going a-milking sir', she said.
'What is your fortune, my pretty maid?',
'My face is my fortune sir', she said.

11

Eventually another milkmaid, called Sarah, came to see Edward about a painful spot on her hand. She said her cow, BLOSSOM, had cowpox and that was where she must have caught her own spot.

Edward decided to make an experiment. He sent for his gardener's son, a young boy called James Phipps. From the spot on Sarah's hand, he took some 'matter', the slightly yellow watery stuff that oozes out of spots. Gently the doctor scratched some of the 'matter' into James' arm. James was very brave and did not cry, even though he was only eight years old.

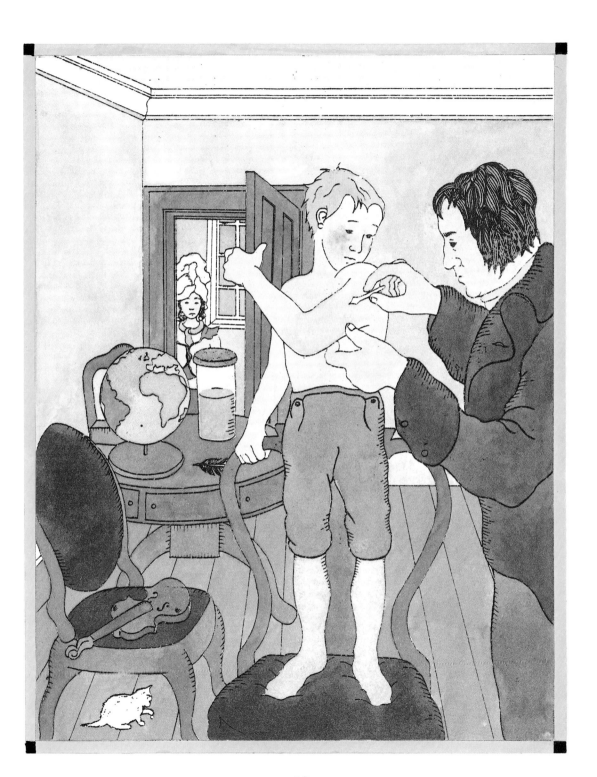

After a few days James felt a bit ill. A spot
appeared where the doctor had made the scratch
and it was quite painful.

But after a few more days the spot had gone and so had the pain. James felt well again. Now Dr Jenner came to the clever part, which was also very dangerous. He wanted to see if James could still catch smallpox.

The doctor went out and found a person with smallpox. This time some 'matter' was taken from the smallpox and scratched into James' arm. Then they waited.

They watched James very carefully. Nothing happened. James had not caught smallpox. He never would, because he was protected just like all the milkmaids. This sort of protection is called IMMUNITY. James was IMMUNE from small-pox.

Everybody was thrilled with the result of the experiment. James was Doctor Jenner's most famous patient and when he grew up he was given a new house. Perhaps it was because he had been so brave. Even Blossom had her picture painted. As more and more people heard about the experiment, she became one of the best known cows in the world.

Doctor Jenner wrote a book about his experiment. Soon people flocked to him to be treated. He sent the cowpox 'matter' (from the spots of people with cowpox) all over the world. It came to be called a VACCINE from the word 'vaccus' which means cow in Latin.

Doctor Jenner was honoured by people all over the world who heard about the smallpox cure and used his vaccine. Indian Chiefs from North America wrote to thank him for saving so many lives in their tribes. People as far away as China and Japan were saved from smallpox.

Doctor Jenner continued to live in the same house in Berkeley for the rest of his life. He went on treating people who lived nearby, and sometimes the line of patients stretched for miles outside his garden gate.

His fame spread across the world. Streets were named after him, he was given medals, and statues were erected in his honour in many countries. There is even a 'Jenner Mountain' in Switzerland. Parliament awarded him a large sum of money which he used to make more vaccine to send around the world.

Quite recently, nearly 170 years after Doctor Jenner's experiment, the World Health Organization decided to try to rid the world of smallpox. It took lots of money and doctors and helpers who worked very hard. They used vaccine from cowpox, just as Doctor Jenner had used on James; they put it into small scratches made in people's skin in the same way, and none of those millions of people then caught smallpox. At last, in 1977 after nearly 20 years of vaccinations in every country, and about 180 years after Doctor Jenner's experiment the world was declared

FREE OF SMALLPOX.

Many other diseases can now be cured by using
VACCINES made in many different ways. Maybe
you have been vaccinated with a different kind of
vaccine to stop you catching measles or polio.

DOCTOR EDWARD JENNER of Berkeley was a great man, but we must not forget, as he would not, that SARAH, JAMES and BLOSSOM played their important parts too.